Preface

Carl Czerny (1791-1857) was born in Vienna, Austria. He was a teacher, pianist, and composer known for his pedagogical works for the piano. He composed a very large number of pieces—more than a thousand pieces—in a variety of genres including masses, choral music, symphonies concertos and chamber music. However, his lasting influence was in his piano studies, which have been greatly esteemed by teachers for generations and are still widely used in piano teaching. Carl Czerny was a student of Ludwig van Beethoven, and was influenced by Muzio Clementi and Johann Hummel.

Note from the editor

25 of the original 100 pieces were selected for this collection. These pieces work well on the harp with minimal changes to the composition.

The pieces are organized based on their level of difficulty for harp students, from the easiest to the hardest. However, the order of the pieces is not absolute. You may find an earlier piece more challenging than a later one. A couple of pieces are harder due to lever changes, but easier if played on pedal harp.

Tempo and dynamic markings, as well as fingerings, are suggestions from the editor.

Kaffee Peck, D.M.A
www.OrangeCountyHarp.com

Born and raised in Malaysia, **Dr. Kaffee Peck** obtained her undergraduate degree in Piano Performance from Oklahoma City University and Doctorate degree in Harp Performance from The Universiy of Sounthern California. In addition of harp, Kaffee has extensive knowledge in piano and classical guitar. As a freelance harpist living in Orange County California, Kaffee teaches many students, collaborate music ensembles, writes and arranges music.

Focused techniques

1. Parallel 3rds   Study 3, 6, 7, 9, 12, 15

2. Parallel 6ths   Study 5, 9

3. Scales   Study 7, 14, 17, 18, 19, 22

4. Alberti bass   Study 14

5. Repeated triads   Study 4, 8, 10, 11, 12, 13, 16, 21, 24

6. 2 against 3   Study 21, 24

7. Dotted rhythm   Study 15, 20, 22, 23, 25

8. Grace notes   Study 10, 23,

9. Arpeggios   Study 15, 17, 18, 19

10. Blocked chords   Study 7, 15, 20, 22, 23

11. Left hand leaps   Study 22

12. Right hand leaps   Study 13

13. Lever changes   Study 10, 16, 17, 18, 19, 20, 21, 22, 23, 25

Note:

Change lever

Change lever only on repeat (2nd time)

Study 1

#2

Carl Czerny

Edited for harp by Kaffee Peck

Study 2

3

Carl Czerny

Edited for harp by Kaffee Peck

Study 3

#4

Carl Czerny

Edited for harp by Kaffee Peck

Andantino

Study 4

5

Carl Czerny

Edited for harp by Kaffee peck

Allegretto

Study 5

#7

Allegretto

Carl Czerny
Edited for harp by Kaffee Peck

Study 6

 # 6

Carl Czerny

Edited for harp by Kaffee Peck

Allegro

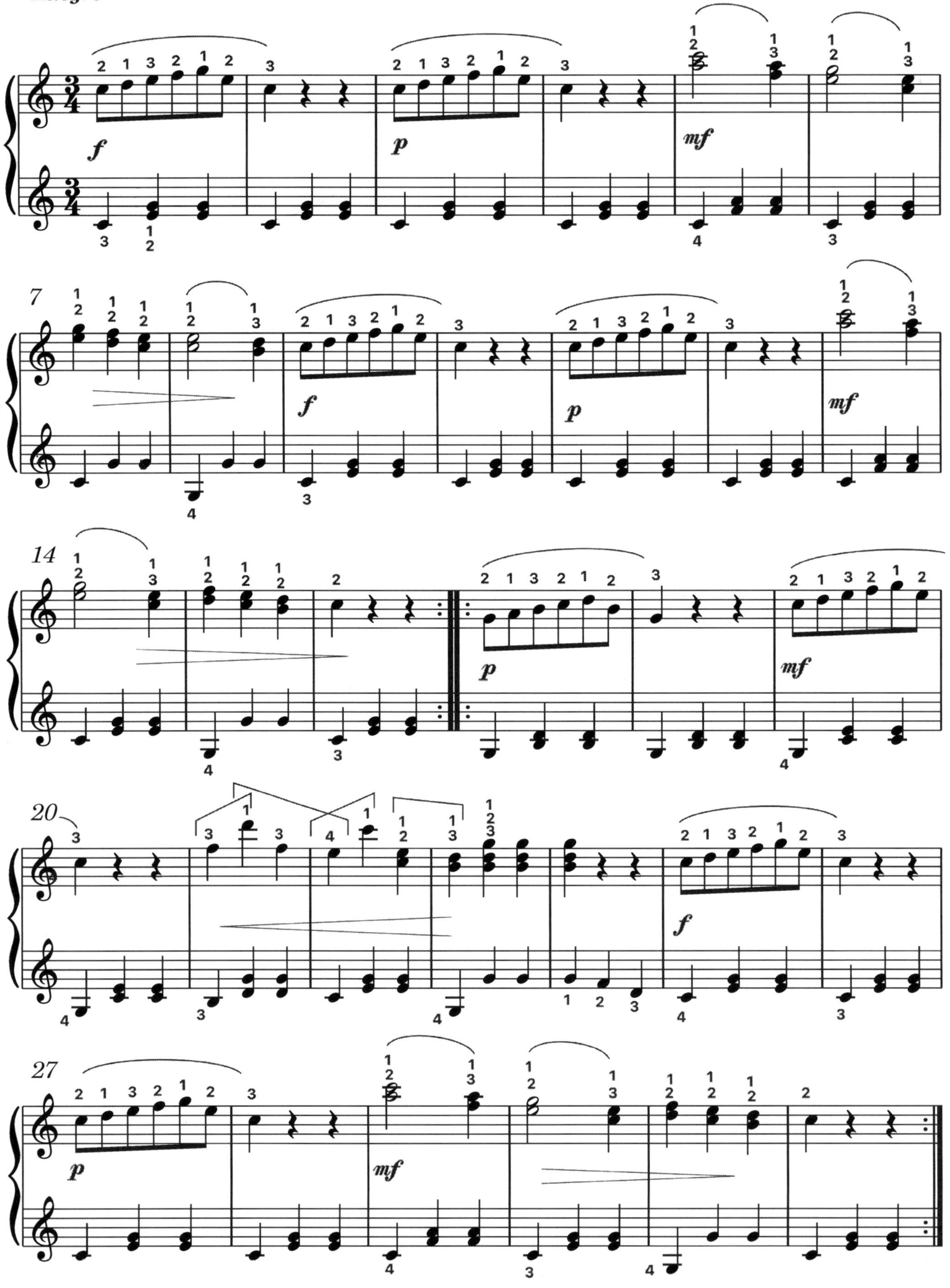

Study 7

#11

Carl Czerny

Edited for harp by Kaffee Peck

Allegro Moderato

Study 8

#13

Carl Czerny

Edited for harp by Kaffee Peck

Allegro

Study 9

 # 16

Carl Czerny

Edited for harp by Kaffee Peck

Andantino

(Left hand can be played an octave higher)

Study 10
#12

Carl Czerny
Edited for harp by Kaffee Peck

Study 10

Study 11

#14

Carl Czerny

Edited for harp by Kaffee Peck

Study 12

#28

Carl Czerny

Edited for harp by Kaffee Peck

Study 13

#22

Carl Czerny
Edited for harp by Kaffee Peck

Study 14

#29

Carl Czerny

Edited for harp by Kaffee Peck

Study 15

#30

Carl Czerny

Edited for harp by Kaffee Peck

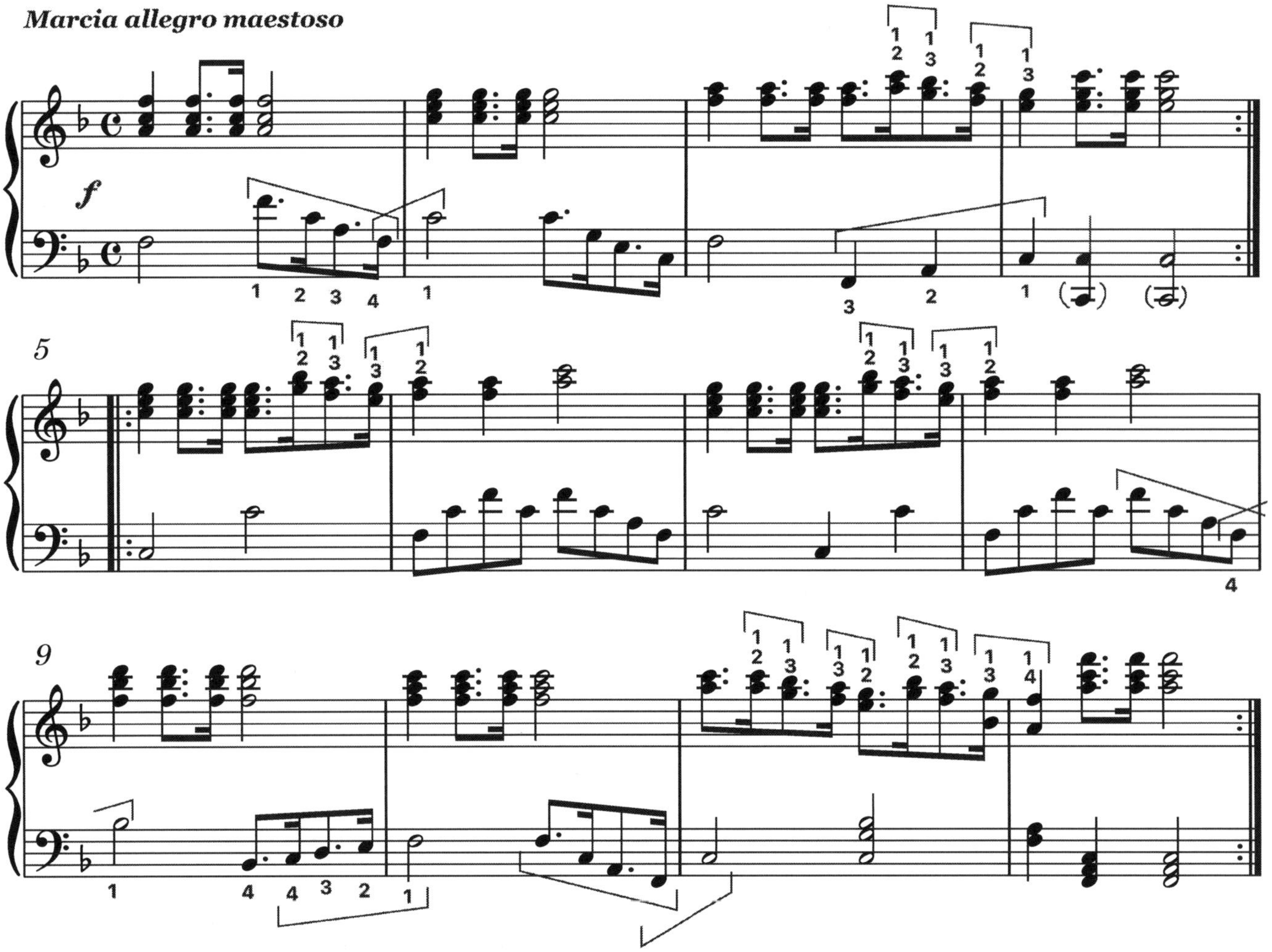

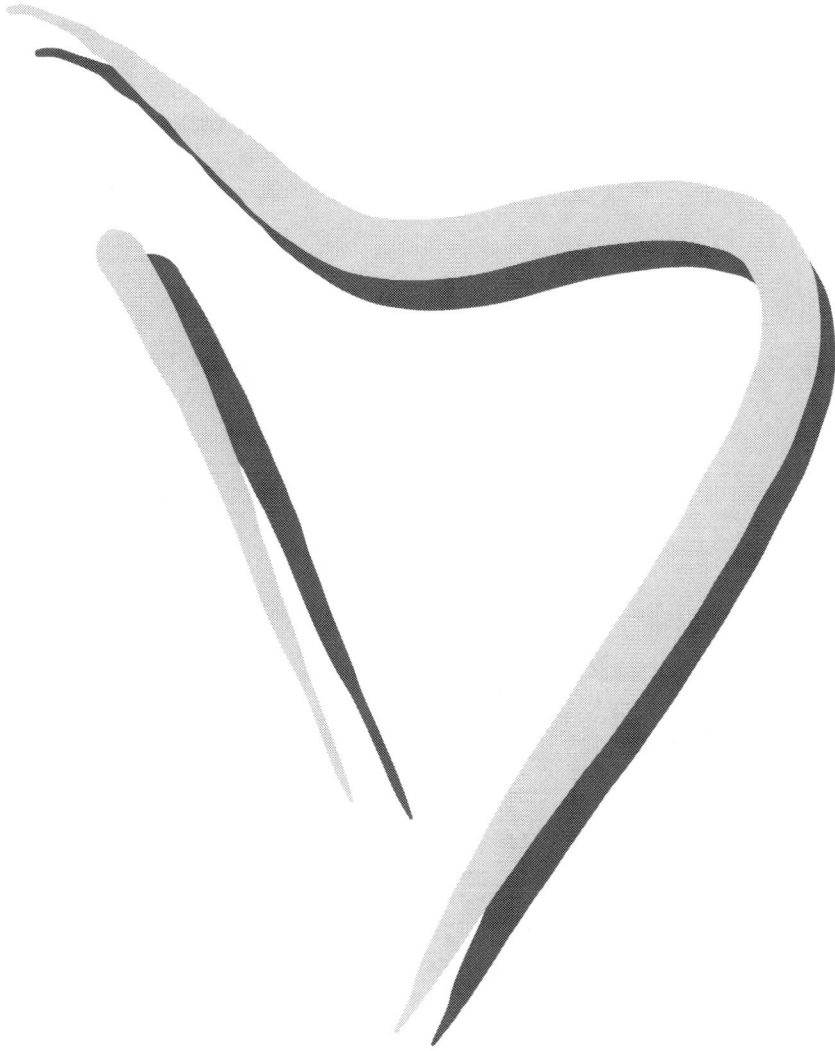

www.OrangeCountyHarp.com

Study 16

#15

Carl Czerny
Edited for harp by Kaffee Peck

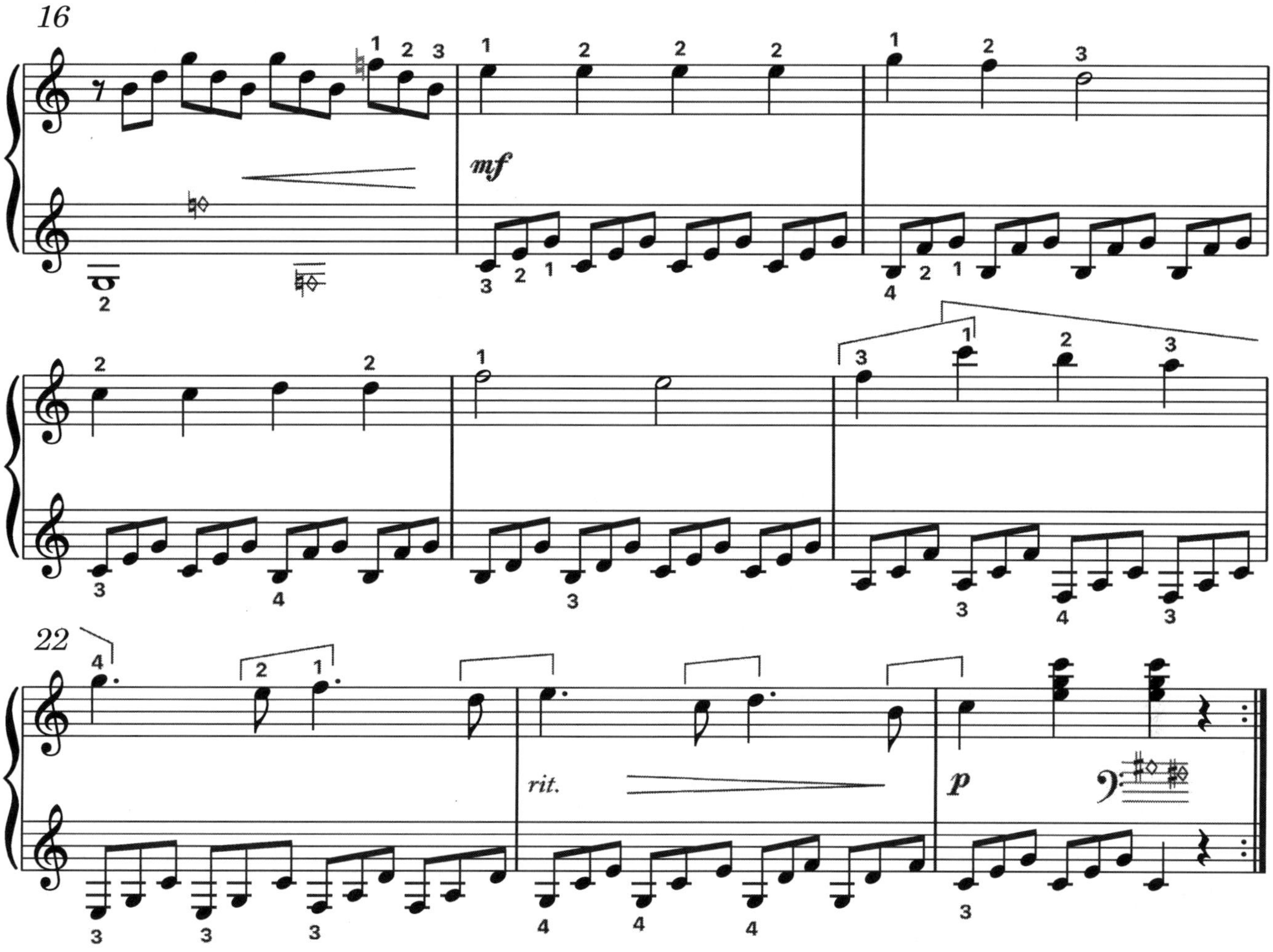
16
mf
22
rit.
p

Study 17

#64

Carl Czerny

Edited for harp by Kaffee Peck

Study 18

#31

Carl Czerny
Edited for harp by Kaffee Peck

Study 19

#36

Carl Czerny
Edited for harp by Kaffee Peck

Study 20

#41

Carl Czerny

Edited for harp by Kaffee Peck

Allegretto

Study 21

#45

Carl Czerny
Edited for harp by Kaffee Peck

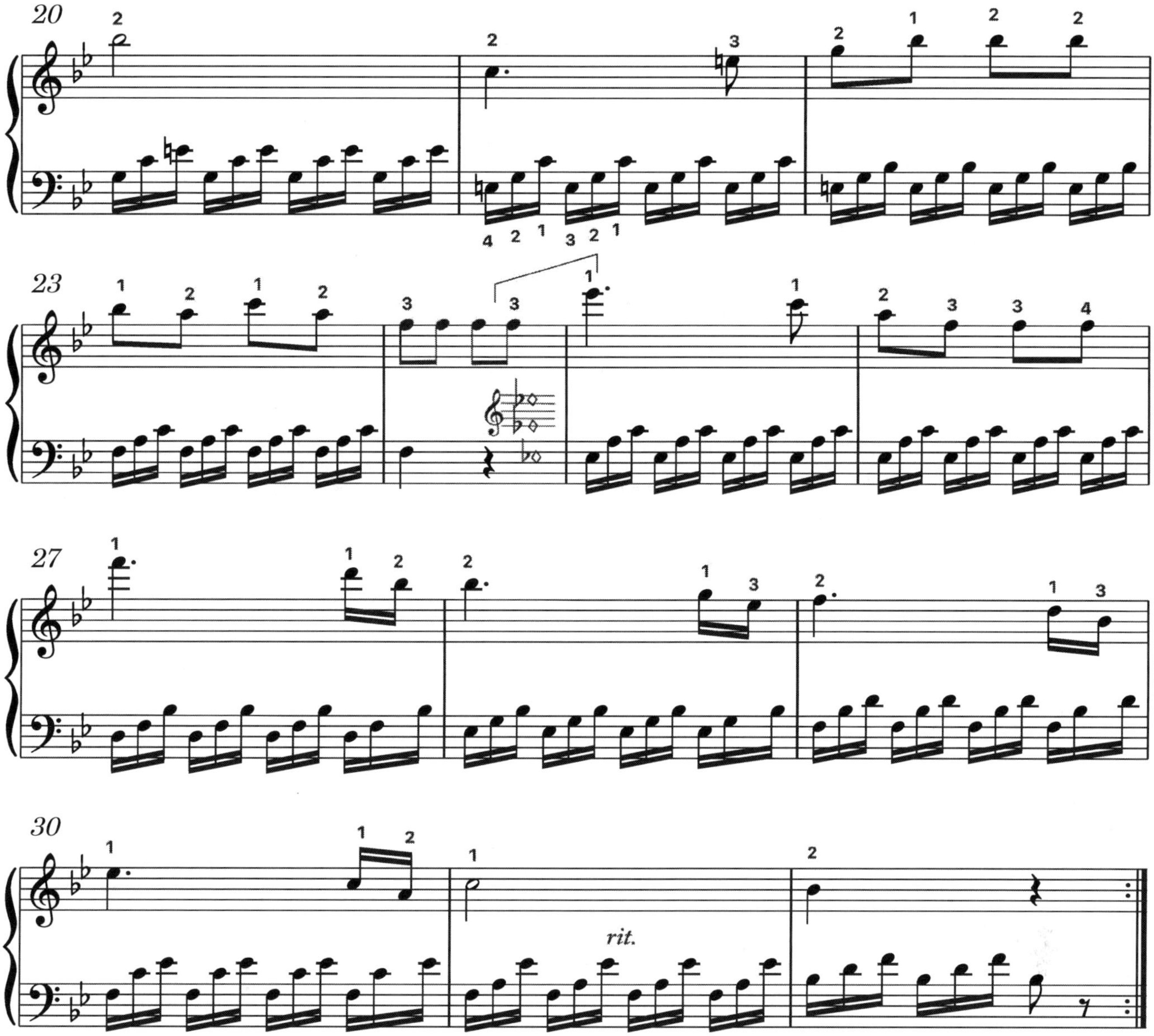
20
23
27
30
rit.

Study 22

#72

Carl Czerny

Edited for harp by Kaffee Peck

Study 23

#52

Carl Czerny
Edited for harp by Kaffee Peck

Study 24
#74

Carl Czerny
Edited for harp by Kaffee Peck

Study 25

#84

Carl Czerny

Edited for harp by Kaffee Peck

Andante

Made in the USA
Las Vegas, NV
21 May 2024